# THE VIEW FROM ZERO BRIDGE

ANHINGA PRESS

# THE VIEW FROM ZERO BRIDGE

Lynn Aarti Chandhok

2006 PHILIP LEVINE PRIZE FOR POETRY

Selected by Corrinne Clegg Hales

ANHINGA PRESS
TALLAHASSEE, FLORIDA 2007

Cover photograph: Vijay Chandhok
Author photograph: Richard Bowditch
Cover design, book design, and production: C. L. Knight
Typesetting: Jill Ihasz
Type Styles: titles and text set in Adobe Jensen Pro

Library of Congress Cataloging-in-Publication Data
*The View from Zero Bridge* by Lynn Aarti Chandhok – First Edition
ISBN – 978-0-938078-98-2
Library of Congress Cataloging Card Number – 2007930850

This publication is sponsored in part by a grant
from the Florida Department of State,
Division of Cultural Affairs, and the Florida Arts Council.

Anhinga Press Inc. is a nonprofit corporation dedicated wholly to the
publication and appreciation of fine poetry and other literary genres.

For personal orders, catalogs
and information write to:
Anhinga Press
P.O. Box 10595
Tallahassee, Florida 32302
Web site: www.anhinga.org
E-mail: info@anhinga.org

Published in the United States
by Anhinga Press
Tallahassee, Florida
First Edition, 2007

*For my parents,*
*Vijay and Shelly Chandhok,*
*who gave me two worlds*

# CONTENTS

# ACKNOWLEDGMENTS

Grateful acknowledgment to the editors of the journals listed here, where these poems first appeared, sometimes in slightly different form:

*The Antioch Review*: "On the Fourth Morning, After Cremation"
*The Dark Horse* (UK): "The Metallurgist's Daughter"
    and "The Carpet Factory"
*The Florida Review*: "Letter to Sargakhet, Kumaon Hills"
    and "Non Sequiturs"
*The Hudson Review*: "Neighboring Planet" and "Hill Sounds"
*The Journal*: "Revision: The Bandh"
*Memorious* (www.memorious.org): "June Morning, Sargakhet"
    and "The Lost Girls"
*The Missouri Review*: "The Bandh," "Lesson," "Mary," "The View from
    Zero Bridge," and "Artemisia"
*The New Republic*: "Still Lifes"
*Prairie Schooner*: "Field Trips with My Daughters,"
    "Brooklyn Botanic Garden, 10/01," "Across Two Continents,"
    "At Shivpur," "Transgression," and "On Yom Kippur
    (Five Meditations)"
*Sewanee Theological Review*: "Eggs Burn Down House, Mother in Bar"
*The Southwest Review*: "Confetti, Ticker-tape"
    and "Inside the Carpet Factory"
*Spoon River Poetry Review*: "The Story of the Palace"
*Tin House*: "Marketplace" and "Phul Chunan"

    "The View from Zero Bridge" was featured on Poetry Daily (www.poems.com) on February 8, 2006 and included in *Poetry Daily Essentials 2007*.

    "Confetti, Ticker-tape" and "Inside the Carpet Factory" received the 2006 Morton Marr Poetry Prize from *The Southwest Review*.

    "Marketplace," "Muharram at 203 Jor Bagh," and "The Story of the Palace" received a Distinguished Entry award in the 2006 Campbell Corner Prize contest and appear on the Campbell Corner web site.

Some of these poems, in different forms, appeared in the chapbook "Picking the Flowers" (Aralia Press).

"The Story of the Palace" was runner-up for the 2006 *Spoon River Review* Editor's Prize.

I am inspired by and indebted to my extended family in India, especially my aunts, uncles, and cousins (in every generation) who have cared for me so well over the years.

For reading this work, for valuable criticism, and for invaluable support, my deep gratitude to Jana Eisenberg, Kevin Roth, Elizabeth di Guglielmo, Bryan Goluboff, Nell Mermin, Carol Graham, Rachel Koenig, Kim Larsen, Lisa Holton, Terri Witek, Bill Coyle, Charles Martin, Greg Williamson, Joshua Mehigan, David Mason, and especially Andrew Hudgins, who has been a true mentor. My unending thanks to Manoj Mehra — my guide in the Kumaon hills and dear friend — who took me to so many beautiful, quiet places. *Dhanya-vād* to Umed Singh Negi and his family. I have been blessed with the love and support of Nancy Holodak (for so many years), and Catherine Bohne, who read everything first and made me want to keep going.

I am grateful to my teachers at the 92nd Street Y, the West Chester Poetry Conference, and the Sewanee Writers' Conference; to Mark Garstein; to Elissa Schappell and Rob Spillman at *Tin House* and Gerry Cambridge at *The Dark Horse* for publishing me early on; to Michael Peich at Aralia Press; to Poly Prep, especially Bill Williams, for a leave of absence years ago that enabled me to begin this project; John Rankin for a summer grant so I could finish it; and Helen Vislocka for her patience and kindness.

My sincere thanks to the faculty and students in the M.F.A. program at Cal State Fresno, especially Corrinne Clegg Hales, for honoring me by selecting my manuscript, and to Rick Campbell and Lynne Knight at Anhinga Press for their wisdom and expertise in helping me turn it into a book.

Rob, Meena and Priya — my true loves — thank you for letting me slip away to write this.

# JUDGE'S NOTE

It's the rich physicality of these poems that draws me to them, and it's their large reach that keeps me coming back. This is a poetry that embraces the problem of distance — geographical, chronological, religious, cultural — and the book gathers quiet force as it weaves between worlds as seemingly distant as Kashmir and Brooklyn, childhood and parenthood, sensuality and intellect, science and tradition. It's a delight to read a new book of poems that not only sings with a beautiful voice, but sings with remarkable wisdom, and sings to the heart.

— *Corrinne Clegg Hales*
*Judge, 2006 Philip Levine Prize for Poetry*

*Ah, but words on the page aren't the whole story*
*for all my hopes and fears are fictions too*
*and I live in a virtual fever of creation —*
*the whole course of my life has been imagination,*
*my days a dream; when we wake from history*
*may we find peace in the substance of the true.*

      — Derek Mahon
        from "Roman Script"

# THE VIEW FROM ZERO BRIDGE

# MARKETPLACE
*Kashmir, 1999*

The clattering horse-drawn carriages, the horns,
the hawkers all fall silent in the flash,
then chaos rises, shattering paradise.
My loss is trivial: a childhood home
to which return would be a senseless risk
just to confirm that paradise was real.
True, even as a child I understood
that bitterness had bled into the earth
beneath the dahlias, leached into the roots
of zinnias, marigolds, to murky lakes
where lotus lay, flat-leaved, blooming in bright
profusions out of quiet pools. I knew
that past the ridge we climbed that August day
to find a hidden lake one might mistake
for sky itself, beyond this, nestled down
between the peaks were border guards, two bands
of men who, facing off, kept peace: the peace
men fought for, not the other peace — the one
we found that day along the mountain ridge,
the air distilled, the silence cooled by clouds;
the peace that let the glaciers age unmoved,
and painted Himalayan peaks in grays
that shifted off the setting sun to blue;
the peace that marked the end of evening prayer,
the ancient song drawn down to whispering
*Om shanti, shanti, shanti, om.*

We've moved away. Though the borders haven't changed
for more than fifty years, we can't forget
the train cars burned — a body for a body.

On either side, the only truth is loss,
and blame is strewn like wreckage or debris,
the storylines, disputed maps, redrawn.

# THE BANDH
*Kashmir, 1970*

The Jhelum River snaked past our back yard,
beyond the corn, the rows of ripe tomatoes —
where mornings we filled baskets, or our skirts,
ran home and begged the cook to make us soup —
past brimming orchards of sweet apples, thick
groves of gnarled plum trees dangling black-skinned fruit.
The Bandh protected us from springtime floods
but blocked our view — built up so high the land
seemed like a shallow basin, till the day
we tucked ourselves between the barbed wire lines
and clambered up the dusty zigzag path,
up to the Bandh's high crest. For the first time,
I saw what stretched out on the other side:
a scattering of huts and smoldering fires,
smoke rising without the scent of prayer or food,
the river ambling, quiet, almost looming,
its current strong enough to wash away
the women who unwound themselves from yards
of saffron sarees, pounding out the silt,
then stretching crimson rivulets of silk
to dry, billowing on the shore — or else
the green-eyed children who would point and laugh,
their quick, white smiles grabbing the evening light —
even the goats and cows that claimed the path
and, edging us aside, clanged home at dusk.
That summer I learned *bandh* meant *closed.* I turned
the grammar over in my head. From here,
the view was clear. The setting sun laid pinks
across the river and the vale. Immense
chinar trees draped their boughs in silhouette.
Then we were silhouette against dim light,

our shadows thin as shadows cast beneath
a gauze of silk or smoke — and no less true.
*The Closed*, I thought, and turned back from the view.

# MARY

I come to watch her grind the cardamom
and cumin seeds, to hear them crackle, roasting
in iron pans. She wipes stray tears and portions
the onions minced with heavy, tarnished knives.
Each mound's a promise: *saag, panir piaz ...*
The seeds have scented her. Her nimble hands
become the seasoning for roots and greens
she slices fine and simmers, feeding me.

She tucks her cotton saree at the waist.
It's threadbare, handed down. I know the silks
are saved for me, but I don't care. I want
just this: the slow demand of daily bread.
At Mary's feet, I learn the words I need,
the words for food, enough to get along.

# A STOLEN DANCE

We're in the back yard before dinner,
sitting with Moti, the chickens,
the cows and the cow dung. The pasture
deepens as twilight sets in.

She's snapping the ends off of green beans,
the bowl resting light on the hammock
her emerald saree becomes
across her invisible thighs.

My brother, the charming one, smiles,
and, taking a chance, steals the bowl.
He lifts her and waltzes her madly
through dusk's strange, diminishing light.

We're making the music. She's laughing
and spinning — her bare feet just graze
black walnuts and thorns that are hiding,
I know, in the grass. *This boy's crazy —*

She frees herself, dizzily grabbing
the bowl I had hidden, wipes tears
she examines on cracked, tender palms,
and whispers *Don't tell Bhabiji —*

# LESSON

At Shalimar, we made the gardener cry.
We raced through mazes trimmed in marigold,
past dahlias, calla lily, climbing rose.
The tight-edged paths contained our games at first,
but soon we clipped the royal beds, ran faster —
smashing the courtly gold and purple blooms.

He didn't chase us off. Instead, he ran
to wake our grandfather, evidence in hand:
crushed petals which he pressed against his face
and then let fall, imploring *please, Sahib, please ...*
My grandfather rose and scolded us, but softly.
And so we learned, like palace princesses,
that he who seemed the master was not our master.
We slowed our steps, minding the paths he tended.

# THE CARPET FACTORY

A wood shack on the riverbank. Inside,
through dust-filled shafts of light, bright colors rise
and drown the warps, transforming their brown threads
to poppy fields, the Tree of Life, a wide
sun hemmed by cartwheeled tulips, fountainheads
that spew blue waterfalls of peacock eyes.

With furious fingers mothlike at the weft,
the children tie and cut and tie and cut
and tamp the knots down, turning blade to gavel.
Each pull's a dust-cloud *plink* — bereft
of music. Toothless men spit betelnut
in blood-red stains. Everywhere, reds unravel.

The bended limbs of saplings twist and part
and weave into the prayer rug's pale silk heart.

# INSIDE THE CARPET FACTORY

At each loom, sitting Buddha-like, there's one
old man who reads the pattern off a scrap
of paper bag he's tucked into the strings.
The penciled letters look like notes. He sings
instructions like a prayer — the *rāg's* a map
of roads that bleed like watercolor, run
the wrong direction, double back, then bloom
into a tree in bloom. The workers hear
the melody as knots, not notes, the line
as dots to be connected. Rows entwine
according to a master plan that's clear
only to the old man — until the loom
recedes, leaving a veil of silk threads bound
by what's unspoken, taking shape from sound.

# THE METALLURGIST'S DAUGHTER

My father's pockets jangled, full of bones
cast in titanium, old keys, a blade
that spun the turbine of a bomber, spools
of gold wire thinner than a human hair,
loose change. But mostly they held supermagnets —
a dime-sized one could hold a whole year's worth
of homework to the fridge. It never slid.

He said the molecules are flat and smooth.
Forged in tight rows, the forces build. Tap them —
they cleave along the lines that give them strength.
I knew this. Still, I couldn't help but play
at holding them apart, then letting go.
They snapped together, shattering on impact.

He'd set them, absent-mindedly, on top
of the TV. Carol Burnett turned green.
The *Born Free* lions gave chase through bright pink grass.

He couldn't fix this, but, trapped in a crowd
of beggar children clamoring for *paise*,
he pulled two magnets from his pocket, held
a girl's thin, outstretched arm, and laid one in
her flattened palm. The other one he rolled
discreetly underneath — and in her hand,
the stone turned somersaults, leapt up and danced.

# THE VIEW FROM ZERO BRIDGE

My father made his way to Zero Bridge
before the sun slipped up the riverbed
and lighted plum groves — long before the cars,
carts, rickshaws, trucks, and bicycles emerged,
dew-slick at dawn, into the dust. He passed
our shuttered shop, passed Ram Bagh Road, arrived
and, with his camera, peered over the edge.
The long *shikaras* jostled side by side,
their pointed noses wedged on the stone slab,
their open bellies full — kohlrabi, beets,
red carrots, long green *kuddu*, string beans — rows
piled patchwork, high as each small boat could hold.
The farmers, barefoot, balanced at the edges,
haggling, counting, weighing. He framed and shot

a young man in an orange, cabled sweater
swinging a bale of okra to his shoulder;
a pyramid of eggplants on a scale;
a farmer setting weights to balance them,
the wind across the Jhelum billowing
his gray pajama. After the shutter closed,
the farmers tipped their heart-shaped paddles, turned,
rowed back to Dal Lake's maze of floating gardens.

It must have been our last year. Had he known,
he might have waited for the shot he missed:
the empty boats, the paddles poised to break
morning's gold film, laid thin across the lake.

# ARTEMISIA

In the dream, I walked the narrow streets
where butchers string up carcasses, but each
dead body was a year I'd been away
staring through hollowed sockets, whispering
*You have no claim. You are no daughter here.*

That day, climbing a spiral staircase, smoke
from artemisia hung in the humid air,
and brought me back to Delhi's cramped bazaars:
the cloying crowds, the eyes dissecting me.
But with the press came longing, too — to hear
the punctual click the *chowkidar's* stick tapped
at night, to taste rosewater syrup, or
feel petals left on marble steps adhere,
turning to stone — to smell the jasmine first
at dawn and then at dusk in my own garden.

The years are real, not corpses, not unkind.
When I return, I'll wind through alleyways
till sense obliterates the dream. And here,
when summer comes, I'll find some marigolds,
pluck off the orange heads and thread them through,
string up the garlands, offerings to time.

# LIVING HERE

# FIELD TRIPS WITH MY DAUGHTERS

## I. Brooklyn Botanic Garden

The rose petal, translucent in late sun,
reveals a web of veins that arc and spread
around themselves like curls of silver wire.
The leaf itself is not what makes us stop
to scrutinize the rose. It is the pale
and unfamiliar insect, pinprick small,
within whose see-through wing the veins are sharper,
tinier, mimicking in shape and grace
the thin veins of the flower on which it feeds.

—∞—

The cacti twist and rise like aliens
or piles of slow, mutating cells. This one,
as tall as two men, thinner than an arm,
arches into a passageway. The limbs
are deeply grooved, reiterating length,
and on each spine, in even spacing, run
long rows of tiny leaves that seem just round
and green, but then, upon inspection, prove
to be small hearts, each hanging on a point.

—∞—

By June, wisteria have come and gone.
their canopy is shade, not color now,
the twisted stalk a calendar of years
each vine has added to itself. We push
against the trunk, expecting solid mass —
instead it swings, so slightly, at our touch.
It's balsa-light, a stage prop. Only leaves
and tangle, not some weight, anchor it here.

## II. Potbellied Seahorse Exhibit, Coney Island Aquarium

*With tails entwined in a nuptial embrace,*
*the female lays 400 eggs. Pouch full,*
the male is left to fertilize and raise
four hundred spindly foals. *She* swims away
to find more unsuspecting males to seed
her eggs. A brief maternal interlude
and she's fulfilled her obligations. Crude
at best, but how much raising could they need?
They're barely living things. They bob and sway
through coral, seaweed, lost in a pink maze
of leaves that, waving, seem more animal
than these unmothered twigs adrift in space.

## III. The Lost Mines, Clay Pit Ponds

Hanging in pale, white clusters like small ghosts,
blueberries flower early. It's barely spring,
and none of spring's bright colors mark this day.
The trees are bare, the sky is faint, not full.
Last autumn's leaves still press against curled roots
in clumps the dull, mild winter left behind.

Collecting catkins from an oak, sweet gum
or birch, or wearing acorn caps on thumbs,
the children scour the path for bugs, and find
raccoon tracks by the stream. A hundred years
ago, they learn, this was a clay pit — mined,
abandoned. Ponds seeped in to fill the holes.
One that was once called Abraham's is now
a field that whispers wishes in their ears.

# TIME'S PARTICLES

I watch the atoms, like confetti, ride
the currents of this house: the crossword tiles
sent flying at the swipe of a cat's paw,
the rain of voices as a girl declares
her presence, says her piece, the wafting dust
and clutter, words that hope to find the page.

The updraft catches one, transforming it
into a Painted Lady, fixing it
upon the wall — it's a transparency,
a child's tattoo applied with water. I
know better than to try to rub it off.

I tuck an atom in my cheek and hope
that it will fix me, too, in time, just like
the homeopath's pill that I once took
to cure me — which would not dissolve. For hours,
time stopped. Then it was gone when I remembered
that I'd forgotten, finally, to look.

# EGGS BURN DOWN HOUSE, MOTHER IN BAR

There she is, drinking gin, wrapping her legs
around a stool, smoking a cigarette
she didn't light. She's completely at ease.
Not far away, the water's boiling down.
But here, nothing's on fire — she's not on fire,
not smoldering. If someone's watching her,
she doesn't see. She doesn't care. The lime
is all she seems to care about, the lime,
not eggs, gone dry, vibrating in the pan.
She sits for hours, laughs, drapes her arm along
a waist — whose waist? — and waits for something — what?
It doesn't matter if it never comes.
Not far away, the eggs expand, hiss. Soon,
the molecules will tear apart. The shells
will fly, and flecks of yolk and white will coat
the ceiling. But in here, it's all intact —
her seamless attitude, the liquid night.
Her fingertips just graze the sweating glass.
She isn't thinking about the eggs at all.

# NON SEQUITURS

I want to tell him it's only bones,
but I know that's not what people say.
They say *bone deep*. They say *cut to the bone*.

I think of this: a hemisphere away,
where parents break their children's perfect bones,
the lineage of beggars carries on.

My body hasn't failed me, though I know
this, too, will come in time. I wait for mine
to twist themselves, to thicken and grow sore
like graceless limbs of dying sycamore
with ugly, dripping knobs. Already now
I sense betrayal looming, worrying
the scaffolding as it begins to fail.

Inheritance, like treason, comes disguised.
I stretch my fingers, check to see which tips
still sit straight, note the one that angles
like a nail hammered wrong — what I have coming.

# REAL NUMBERS
*for my mother*

It took me years to understand: $a^3$
isn't a number, but a cube, a shape
with volume, just a way to measure space.

Once, I believed I knew the shape I'd need
to fill a shapeless void: the embryo,
I thought, amorphous, but ambitious, too —
creates itself as it divides itself.
The product (one) defines identity
within the limits of her gaze — until,
in time, she looks away, creating distance
from its opposite, and redefining "one."
The void returns where solid seemed to form.

Now, even the limit of a curve
makes sense to me, the notion that a line
can move both farther from and closer to
its origin. The girl who walks that line
is heading off to where the arc pulls hard.
She can't yet know that over time (our $y$),
the curve will flatten toward the axis, and
she'll recognize her image coming close
across a chasm, narrowing. She'll see
the distance is no more than this: the thickness
of silver upon glass, what keeps a hand
from reaching its reflection in the mirror.

This math is linear, and moving toward
infinity, two lines will solve for $a$,
dissolving distance, almost, to a point.

# LONG MEADOW

The park is too quiet for August —
not empty, but littered with bodies
at rest in the haze like old cairns
mapping the shade.

In this heat, we're all that's in motion.
My daughters, two renegade moons,
vibrating, spinning around me,
pull me along.

We drop down — too close to a couple
asleep with their backs to us, curled
in a thin, private S. What I want
today is that quiet.

I pull the girls in, start to whisper
wild stories of castles and queens —
I don't want to bother the lovers
who share this brief shade

but the moons slip back out into orbit —
flushed, sweating, too loud, uncontained.
I'm thinking, *I was that girl once*
*in somebody's arms* —

Now the lovers, disturbed by us, stir.
As she rises, she smooths her gray
hair, her old house dress, and smiles
at my girls as they play.

# ORDERS OF MAGNITUDE
*Brooklyn, 2000*

Out too late, on the avenue, I imagine —
or hope for — stars arched over earth like flowers
on darkened branches; satellites that fall
like messengers of old catastrophes;
bright red planets. Any of these would do.
But here, midnight is never broad or black,
the rooflines halve Orion, and the moon
in halo backlights aging cornices.

Once, I climbed switchback paths till trees gave way
to glaciers melting into lakes they fed,
resurfacing as islands, mirror on mirror,
like ice clouds skipping off a soundless sky.
There, nights were brilliant. God seemed plausible.
The cliffs might block the view, the valleys narrow,
but at a turn, it all turned to expanse.
That day, I found myself surrounded, cupped
inside a glacial cradle, while the clouds
unrolled like bolts of quilter's batting, fell
and hid the sky. I sat alone and cold,
a single goatherd's bell in hollow choir,
and waited.
                    Now, walking the avenue,
I know the clouds will lift. I know this too:
Orion cartwheels, vanishing in spring.
Still, I find myself imagining
that city lights might falter, or just dim
one night, till constellations in their full
dimension brighten, as in heaven's view.
That sky might hail some new catastrophe.
At least I'd comprehend its magnitude.

# LOOKING INTO THE FIRE

# MUHARRAM AT 203 JOR BAGH

*New Delhi, April 2001*

I see now why they call them floats — they glide
and hover just above the swarm of men
filling my street tonight, a rising sea
of bodies, torch-fires, smoke, song, drumbeats — high
above them ride the painted cardboard frames,
the portrait hidden under jasmine garlands
and Mylar ribbons glittering gold and green.

I stand inside our gate and watch them turn
into Karbalah Nursery, an open field
they say was once a Moslem cemetery.
I wonder how it happened, how no one saw
the gravestones disappearing, turning to trees.
Even the sacred changes. I've been told,
in years past, on Muharram, celebrants
would lash themselves with branches until they bled.

But not tonight, not yet. They sing and dance
holding aloft the image of the saint
who once was buried — or was it martyred? — there.
I'm not sure of the story, but I've heard
they come each year to dig a giant pit
and toss the floats in, burying him again.

I try to concentrate, to understand
a holiday of lashings, martyrs, graves.
Instead, I find I'm thinking *more of them
than us*, and noticing how thin the lone
policeman is. As if for the first time,
I see the picture windows of our house,
my children fast asleep inside. The lights

announce *we're here alone!* Beneath my hand,
the wrought iron gate is rusted where it latches.

The drumbeats amplify as darkness falls.
I'm not sure any more which way the stream
of men is flowing, or if they'll ever leave.
What sparks a crowd to riot? Suddenly,
a man comes closer, lurches into focus,
gesturing towards my house, excited, shouting —
I try to translate quickly, but I shake
my head, push him back, before I comprehend:

*Madam, my daughter needs to use a bathroom* —
He's gone before I see, or don't see, her
or know which way to look —

                                    a deafening crash
startles the crowd — the current turns to eddies —
screams pitch up, then dissolve —

                                        it's nothing, just
a bank of thunderclouds, months out of season.
The black sky turns pale green and pellets us
with cartoon raindrops round as cannonballs.
The music dies. The crowd evaporates.
By nine, the street is calm, and ours again.

Sweepers come quickly, landing here to purge
all trace of festival — the bits of gold,
chewed *pan*, sticks from kebabs — leaving the dust
in soft, groomed spirals flecked with moon-yellowed leaves.

Before I fall asleep, a bullhorn's call
disrupts the midnight quiet, floating past
to tell us that a seven-year-old girl
was lost in all that. *Only one?* I think.
*In all that, how was only one swept under?*

# THE STORY OF THE PALACE
## *Fatehpur Sikri, April 2001*

*Although the palace and city*
*of Fatehpur are remarkably well preserved,*
*the design and decoration*
*present a problem of interpretation.*


I've been here twice before. Still, their attack
is more than I can stand. Even the book
on Agra says the peddlers here are worse
than anywhere. I grab my girls and curse
my way through outstretched hands — men shouting, "Look!
Look! Lovely bangles!"
                              "Madam likes the black?
This white one? Every color!"
                                        "This for hair?"
"Need film?"
                    "Need toy for baby?"
                                                  Deftly, he's
unveiled a brass wire globe that he untwists —
"See? Ball ... flower ... butterfly ... snake ... bird ...!" He lists
a dozen other shapes. "Just five rupees!"


My daughter is transfixed. She makes me swear:
"We'll get one back in Delhi. *Every* store
on Janpath has them. Sweetie, one of these
won't last ten minutes."
                                    "Mama, please — "
"Look, baby, we don't know these men — you know — "


She turns on one heel, pushes past to go
in through the sandstone gates.

What I expect
inside — lithe minarets, carved deities
watching from every nook, their faces flecked
and scarred by time — seem to have vanished. All
we're looking at is one closed door, a wall,
a single archway. There's no plaque or sign.

"Like Alice," I think, stooping to get through,
only to find another mud-walled room.

—∞—

*Its parts are better than the whole:*
*it lacks, for instance,*
*an orienting spine.*

Flattening the guidebook out, I turn, compare,
and turn. The fine schematic is, at last,
no help: this winding palace is beyond
reduction to a single half-page map.
That's when I hear a voice:
                              "You need a guide?"
I'm outraged (once again), sure I've been spied
on looking lost and fallen in some trap
laid by the hawkers.
                        I look up. A fond
old man in white, with specs of inch-thick glass,
expressionless, almost, is standing there —
where he was not before — as if to say
"You know you need a guide."

Though in my book
it says the guides themselves make up the stories,
that no one knows the purpose of each room —

*... a granary, or else a tomb,*
*explains the lack of windows —*

The girls are waiting. They don't really care
if what this lovely man says *is* a lie.

He takes us through a tiny doorway I
had overlooked, and there's the open plaza,
the archways framing cantilevered halls
that telescope like mirrors tunneling back ...

—⁂—

*The most intriguing building is Panch Mahal,*
*the five-storied Pavilion of the Winds*
*used by the women of the royal household*
*and ladies of the harem —*
*Ruqayya, Mariam, Salima, Jodh Bai —*
*The Christian queen, the Muslim queen, the Hindu ...*

"This courtyard is where the king and queen played chess."
"Parcheesi!" I correct him.
                    "Of course, yes,
the king sat here and moved the slaves around —
live pieces for his game ..."
                    But here's the thing:
A dozen years ago, when I was here,
I climbed up Panch Mahal. The stairs are closed
now. Then, the story was he sat up *there.*

Half-listening, half-nose-down in the pages,
half-watching my two girls, who've run to play
Parcheesi with themselves, posing as pawns,
I hear him say (quite certainly), "The school
was over there, and there, the ministers
gave counsel to the king." Off to my right,
two laborers are carting hunks of stone
from underneath a dry reflecting pool.

—⁂—

*An excavation was undertaken*
*for which no rationale was given.*
*The findings were so announced*
*to give the impression that the Jain*
*images discovered were destroyed*
*by Muslim rulers like Akbar …*

"Anup Talao — the government believes
this site was built on by the Jains, before
Akbar arrived." I watch the pool unfill
wondering what, next time we visit, he'll
proclaim as we regard the watery blurs
that are ourselves.
                    My young pawn turns and shouts,
"What happens to the slave girls at the end?"
"Good question," I reply, then, winging it,
"This king is good. He lets them play again."

—⁂—

*The underlying structure is Hindu post-and-beams,*
*in many cases roofed with Muslim vaults and domes …*

The noon sun's hot, and there's no wind.
I call the girls and step inside
a darkened room I don't recall
from last time. Lining every wall,
red sandstone's carved in complex shapes —
stars, diamonds, swastikas — arranged
in some sure scheme. I need the guide.

"Akbar's great vision. He believed
the world's religions all held truth.
That centerpiece is for King Solomon —
And there! The stars of David —
swastikas for the Hindu faith —
Shiaz, four pointed stars, and there —
Shi'ite, Jain, Christian, everything —
'Din-I-Elahi' — he conceived
a new religion, the best parts
of each joined on one path ..."

Beneath the jali-work are scenes
of animals and birds, flowers, trees.

"Akbar knew that when faith began,
flora and fauna were, to man,
the most, *most* holy."
                  But the faces
have all been scraped away, and in their places
black smudges mark where hands have looked for them.

"Akbar's great-grandson, Aurangzeb.
He ordered that the faces be removed
in keeping with the principles of Islam."

*There never would have been carved deities.*

We touch the spaces too, as if compelled,
then move along.

               "And here is where the son
Akbar had prayed so long for, for an heir,
was born — "
             The girls pipe up. "A baby? Where?"

"For years his wives had all been barren. Then,
with one saint's blessing, Jahangir was born
and Akbar built this city to celebrate
the son who would carry out what he had started."

A cloud of parrots smokes up from the shadow
of a lone cypress bent by long-lost winds.

—⁓—

"This city flourished fourteen years, and then ..."

*Akbar left to defend the western borders —*
*It turned out that the ground here held no water —*

The book says one thing. Our man says another.

He checks his watch, and so I pay the guide
a little extra too, though I'm not sure
I trust a word he said. He disappears
into the swarm of peddlers whose bright spheres
keep magically transforming in their hands.

I pull ten rupees from my bag, "For two."
At least the girls are quiet, satisfied
they know who-ate-what-where and when and who-
killed-so-and-so —

        "Mom, look what I can do!"
She's turned the wire into a golden crown.
"I'll be the queen ..." and she begins her tale.

—⁓—

As it recedes, the palace takes the pale
cast of the picture on the guidebook cover.
The plains are dry as ever, but the land's
dotted with cypress, neem, and tufts of green
just like in Indian miniatures I've seen
where gods come down to chase a mortal lover.

# CONFETTI, TICKER-TAPE

I want to say they're swallows. In September,
when we were feeding everyone we could,
we'd look for them above the tracks on Ninth Street.
What startled me was how their undersides
caught the light, flashed silver, how the group
would swoop and rise like wind itself, the flock
vanishing every time it changed directions,

how the birds hung on air and clung together
circling above us, silver, like the squares
we thought were bits of fuselage or flakes
of skyscraper, falling, until they floated
towards us, lower, landing on our front stoop
and I picked the papers up, but they were blank —
one after the other, blank, burned at the edges.

# BROOKLYN BOTANIC GARDEN, 10/01

Today, I come alone to get my bearings,
but in "Aquatics" everything's afloat:
Lily pads large as hammocks, amethyst flowers,
pond scum and weed so thick, I start to think
I could walk across it, but the railing
and cold, black water peeking through the reeds
remind me *what seems permanent will change …*

Inside this room of lakes and foliage
someone imagined, then drew up in plans,
a woman paints the lily pads, the flowers
that dangle overhead — a decoupage
of pinprick stars, or stage lights clipped to wires.
She paints the hothouse world as if it's not
already art, or dream, or plan, or real.

# ON YOM KIPPUR (FIVE MEDITATIONS)
*Brooklyn, 2001*

Maybe it's just the walk itself I want.
The fifteen blocks alone in echoing light
could do as much as any house of god.

Across the street, an old sardarji strolls
beside his son, as if out of some film —
as if I'm watching now — his crimson turban
bobbing against the evening's amber tones.
The son's a shadow of his father — shaved,
short-haired, and turban-free. The outline blurs
until I see I'm looking at myself.

—⁊⁊—


Inside, I find a balcony spot and flip
through prayer books looking for the one they're on.
Below me, white shawls, covered heads — a scene
that should seem foreign, but I know this noise —
unmuffled conversation, song and chant
and children crying, like in Delhi, where
sitar and tabla rippled back and forth,
the audience an instrument — *ah! ah!* —
in conversation with the *rāg*. So here,
the song's almost familiar, but not quite.

—⁊⁊—


An hour later, lost in the rising prayers,
I thumb through the translations, as if these —

set down eight hundred years ago — might yield
some answer. Then they do: the prayer's a puzzle.
I picture an old rabbi, veiled in sound,
his life spent rearranging letters till
the prayer returned to alphabet and then
unraveled into strings of words that wound
themselves to God, acrostically. I'm thrilled,
and then dismayed. This proves my fears —
born centuries late (perhaps to the wrong sex),
I've missed my calling: puzzle-master, priest
in charge of letters, patterns, "sounds-like" games —
one left alone in candle-lit rooms to play
with fragments, phonemes, the parts of what we are.

—∿—

Earlier, on the same day, we picked apples
from trees far too voluptuous (obscene
almost) to be believed, but they were real.
Apple fought apple for a bit of branch
to cling to, then held fast. They didn't budge
through weeks of ripening. No breeze swayed them.
On one, an equally unmoving leaf
had cast the image of itself in green —
a pinhole camera: apple skin as film.
It made me think of Hiroshima, how
the victims closest to the blast left not
their carcasses but shadows on the wall.

Now, sitting in the temple, I can't think
of anything else that's like that silhouette
or conjure up a god whose hand, at once,
could be as heavy and as light as this.

The walk is three blocks down and twelve across,
past rows of brownstones joined by party walls
where conversations rise and slip through cracks
and float like cartoon bubbles, but the words
fade out to scattered sounds *(ah, ah!)*, too faint
to make out in the dark. The streetlights cast
their shadows down in shapes that correspond
to something, but I can't tell what. This light's
illuminating nothing, empty squares
that look like crossroads, crosswords. In my path,
a long, dark line gets shorter, shorter, till
I underline myself. I turn toward home
(three down, a place, four letters). After me,
the shadow lengthens, thins, and slips away.

# ORDINARY CITIZENS

"Express" is not a promise. We all know that,
so no one seems surprised the number four
is inching through the dark below Canal.
At least the car's not too full, just young moms
with lots of kids, guys off the early shift,
some bank tellers on lunch, and at the far
end of the car, a standard-issue drunk:
wild wiry hair, a crumpled paper bag,
muttering just too much to be ignored.

Someone yells, "You! Shut up!" Another guy,
deciding he's been wronged, stands and declares,
"I'm just an ordinary citizen!"
then maypoles through the crowd to find the drunk,
shouting, "I gotta listen to you curse?
Well, fuck. I'm just an ordinary guy,
riding the fucking train." (He doesn't get
his own joke.) He stops before they're face to face
and boasts, "I'm gonna hurt someone today.
You wanna tell me who it's gonna be?"

The drunk recoils, then takes a swig, straightens up
and spits, "Fuck you."
                        Outside, the tunnel brightens,
but it's a local stop. The doors stay shut.
The rest of us press up against the doors
as if there's some imaginary line
of fire we can avoid. The men remain
at arm's length, cursing and staring. Someone says,
"He's crazy," but I can't tell who she means.

At last, the train slows, and the doors sigh open.
The men slip off together, poised to fight.
We seem to wait here much too long, but when
we finally move, they're still there on the platform.
The crazy one has taken out a chain.

He swings it around his head as we roll past,
and like a child attempting double-dutch,
the other one is focused on the arc,
waiting to strike. And then it all goes dark.

# TRUST

We've pulled it off again. The presents finished,
my daughter asks, *Is Santa still awake?*
I promise her he's watching, so she looks up —
as if he's on the ceiling — and says *thank-you.*

The whole year I was eight, I dreamed that fires
rained down from blooming mushroom clouds, rose up
and raced toward me in bed. I had been told
that this could happen. Now, I never dream
of fires, and wouldn't dream of telling her
how fast they spread from one place to another.

I can't explain that old, this new, disaster,
and I'm undone by what children believe:
the ones who dream of martyrdom, or mine —
who trust that what I tell them is the truth.

# THE NEWS
*June 2002*

Eighteen today. A car bomb, somewhere, *where?*
In California, a lover's letter ignites
a thousand times a thousand acres, until
we don't know whether to pity or hate the lover
who sparked the flame, now raging out of control.

*It isn't hard to picture her, the page*
*at arm's length, with the edges turning black,*
*blooming and disappearing till the words*
*evaporate. It seems so easy. She*
*can't tell if she let go or if the wind*
*just took the last of it out of her fingers,*
*setting the cinders loose in all that air.*

—⚡—

Was it like this for them that day? Did they
look deep into the fire, careering forward,
close to the edge, the end, and then surrender?

## STILL LIFES

*after two paintings by Richard Baker*

Taking their final breath, the tulips strain
against blue glass, against a window pane,
like glowing Tussaud ladies. The pink heads twist.
The whole arrangement almost levitates
except where fading leaves curl, darkening
the edges like the lips of half-burned candles.

Light shifts across the room. This palette handles
bouquets of mackerel tossed on shallow plates,
mouths open, hopeful, a foliage of tails,
dead, glassy eyes, the crenulated scales.
These fish are solid stuff, no pointillist
illusion, no "Table with Food." The silver hardens.

Behind the house, the alley, city gardens,
a frieze of clouds. A hundred windows frame
a hundred insides looking out, the dry
collage of bricks, fire escapes shadowing
bare branches pointed skyward with the same
strained prayerful attitude against the sky.

# NEIGHBORING PLANET

*"What crowd is this?"*
— *William Wordsworth*

He must be here tonight. There's a small crowd
of subway riders, just emerged, like me,
at Ninth Street, murmuring, "No — it's free … "

                                          I'll wait,
though I should be getting home. I've seen the news:
Mars will never be this close again.

A couple leaves, rejoining hands. "It's red,"
they whisper, thrilled. "No, *really* red." Last time,
when he had Saturn in his sights, I said,
"Exactly like the rings in all the books,"
or something equally brilliant, to the guy
behind me in the line.
                         When it's my turn
he points out, first, up by the park, but low,
a faintly orange star, then tells me how
to hold my eye, just so, above the eyepiece
until I see — dark valleys, smooth red seas —
jostling a bit, but "just like in the pictures — "
There I go again, confirming — what?

"It's really nice of you," is what I mean,
and say, though, pleased or proud, he doesn't show it.
He just turns to the next person in line
and points up toward the park. I turn toward home,
now satisfied, now with grave, steady joy
in this great thing, so bright, and not so distant.

ACROSS TWO CONTINENTS

# REVISION: THE BANDH

The women don't wear sarees in Kashmir.
Whose memory is this? Why did I write it?
Was it a dream or vision that such lengths
could spread themselves, so beautifully, on the banks?

Driving now to Kumaon hills, we pass
the fabric factories. All around us, fields
are spread with drying sarees: indigo
and saffron, mustard, lavender, like ribbons
but tethered to the dry, cracked earth and stretched
by hot plains wind. Could it have been this scene?
Or was it in a film on Varanasi?
The long shot of the river: Death floats past,
but still the women, silhouettes on gold,
pound out the day against the rocks, unfurling
the banners they'll use to wrap themselves tomorrow.

# ON THE FOURTH MORNING, AFTER CREMATION

*i.m. Prakash Vati Chandhok, 1914-1989*

The men do this: Remove their shoes. Step down
the long gray stairs into the ash. Wade in
and run their fingers through to find, still warm,
the pieces of her bones that have endured.
Collect the fragments. Fill a burlap sack —
not large — it might hold rice or flour if not
these bones. Scoop handfuls of rose petals, soft
as ash, into the bag. Then tie it up.

For hours, drive the road along the river.
Look to the cold, worn landscape. Find the spot,
the clearing where the river's arc casts back
the daylight. Disembark. Remove their shoes.
Roll up their pantlegs to the knees. Wade in
across the stones to where the current's swift
but tender. Balance and untie the bag.
By handfuls, place her gently on the water.

And I do this: Stand on the shore and strain
to see. Compelled, unbidden, I remove
my shoes, and roll my pants, and gingerly
negotiate the river and its stones.
I'm taken in. I do not cast the bones
but watch as, with the petals, she departs.
She travels fast, her stiffened body gone.
The petals dance upon the surface, flash
then flicker, undiminished, in my eye.

# EVERYTHING RISES

We hear the news. Words fail. With nothing else,
my father asks me if I'd like some milk.
I heat it and I sit with him. It's late.
He says, "The taste is different here."
I say, "The smell, too." After a while, he asks
if I remember when we hiked to Yusmarg.

He went in '46, into the woods,
arranging lumber shipments. Where he slept,
the fields were purple — filled with short, dark flowers.
*The smell was so intense, we dreamed wild dreams*
*and woke to milk that tasted just like thyme.*

We laugh about the cows. The house turns quiet.
Outside, black hills and Himalayan sky
merge to a darkened canvas, dotted now
with floating cottage lights and falling stars.

# PHUL CHUNAN

*i.m. Anisha Dang, 1972-2003*

At the cremation grounds, your father holds
my hand and says, *On my veranda, late*
*at night, I'd hear the wind chimes that she hung*
*and think, "My daughter is so beautiful."*

Behind him, priests are washing off your bones
so loudly that I barely hear the rest —
*I never climbed the stairs to tell her so.*

When someone hands me marigolds, I take
my turn and drop them in the bright bronze urn.
The lid is closed. The ribbon seems too red.

At Gangotri, where they'll finally let you go,
the marigolds will mark your progress, bright
like grace notes on the current, like the words
I wish I'd heard, or wish I could have spoken.

# ACROSS TWO CONTINENTS

I'm farthest at the moment when the phone
rings at the wrong hour. Even if we leave
today, it's their tomorrow. It's too late.
I'm only witness through the eyes of others:

*Three hundred people came to touch his feet. …*
*We dressed her in her wedding saree, washed*
*her by ourselves, put flowers in her hair. …*
*She was so young. Even I couldn't bear it.*

And then I think it's better not to know.
We shouldn't travel. Or we should have stayed.
Here, we might wait for days after a death
while someone, somewhere, stores an empty corpse.
There, time moves quickly. Bathing and then burning,
we let them go, but only from our hands.

# AT SHIVPUR

*i.m. Jai Dev Chandhok, 1907-2003*

This time, I take the ashes and the bones
in both my hands and hold them. It's raining,
and we're knee-deep in the Ganges, soaked
to the skin, and holding him who has none.
The bones are hollow, gritty, and so many,
as if a thousand birds had crashed in flight,
the impact burning up their flesh and feathers.
I watch my father pick these flowers, hold
one in his hands, examine it for signs
of where it's been, what function, but his tears
spare him the recognition. Standing here,
placing the bone and ash upon the surface,
I let the current take them, and I look
to see the petals flash against the gray.
Instead, the rain comes harder. Everything blurs.
I rub my hands together in the water,
then climb the gravel bank, grabbing a stone —
pitted and flecked with quartz — to carry back.

# TRANSGRESSION

I'm told it isn't done, that it's bad luck
to bring the ashes back inside the house.

So, keeping some to carry home — abroad —
is bound to bother someone. I can hear
the Customs man now: "Ma'am, what's that gray powder?"

I do it anyway. It seems important
though he'd been in my garden only once,
before it was a garden really. Still,
he'd blessed it.
                    There, we only leave the dust
to rivers, never earth. But I suppose
transgression takes whatever form one needs
to satisfy a longing or a hunger
or disappointment: he had come so close
to living what, to me, seemed like forever.

The time is never right. The cotton bag
hangs like forgotten groceries on the doorknob
all winter. I proclaim the ground "too cold,"
though we'd dispersed his bones in icy water.

In spring, my daughter helps me spread the ashes,
singing, "It's going to make the flowers more lovely."
And I believe it does. The bleeding hearts,
as hackneyed as it sounds, *do* overrun
the sweet alyssum and the ferns. Even when
I clip them to the stalks, they bloom again.

It's months before I notice that the bag's
still hanging, empty, from the kitchen doorknob.
I realize I can't touch it, though I think
I'll take it to the hills someday. The sun
will bleach it perfect white like those small flags
next to the mountain temples. Soundless wind
will rearrange it, lift it, and, in time,
unwind the edges to a prayer shawl's fringe.
In time, then. But the time is never right.

ON THE NEW LAND

# JUNE MORNING, SARGAKHET

The dawn comes earlier here. I rise with it
easily, rested, even though the night
brought armies through my dreams, wave after wave:
the monsoon wind first, tearing the branches loose,
hurling them to the roof, then swooping down
to work the roof itself free from the eaves.
And then the rain, for hours, its thrash and thrum
a raging heartbeat telling me some truth
about the heart, unmeasured, unrestrained —
how frightening it can sound, and comforting
at once. Even the calm that settled in
after the rain loomed like a worried truce
until, before the dawn, two small gray birds
stole the last crumbs of quiet from the sill.

None of this has disturbed me. I awaken
to watch fog climb the hillside, angled light
fracture the open doorway, where a string
of marigolds turns to a string of jewels.
Anywhere else, I'd miss the laughing thrush
calling his mate, ignore the blue-tipped plume
a black bird shed. Here, time slows till the bee
no longer swerves and darts but finds some rest
on fronds of saffron-spiked crocosmia,
uncurls a black straw, drinks. On the same stalk,
a silvering drop hangs somehow undisturbed.
I watch for hours. These hills ask for no more
than what they offer: silence, passion, sense,
storm and then quiet, all risked, all set right.

# A CONVERSATION WITH THE GUIDE

On the way to Kapileshwar, when you asked
about my gods, I said I thought the walk
itself proved something, that some unseen hand
must have arranged the forest canopy.
Here in the hills, I thought my proof quite sound,
but you said you felt God inside the temples
or at cremation grounds.
                                    We came to both:
Kapileshwar rising where two rivers merged;
along the banks, pyres that had burned out days
or weeks before. We made our way across,
removed our shoes, stooped at the low-hung door,
and crawled inside the thousand-year-old room —

unlit, damp-walled and cramped, but something kin
to stone cold country churches. When my eyes
adjusted, the colors came as offerings —
marigold, rhododendron, lilac, jasmine.
Someone before had poured milk on the stones,
left rice, left incense, still lit, smoke still curling.

I moved to the far corner, sat cross-legged,
tried not to watch you pray, then tried to pray.
A thousand years of voices listened in
to what we thought, oil burned, and goddesses,
anointed with the oranges of Holi,
kept to their gentle vigil. Overhead,
a hundred brass bells hung in silence, strung
so tightly it seemed time itself was bound.

We stayed for hours, left too late, barely spoke —
caught in a calm that pooled like wind-swept leaves,
and not because the dead lay all around.

Climbing away, I turned for one last look
at stone on stone, impossibly at ease,
keeping safe watch over what my gods had made.

# LETTER TO SARGAKHET, KUMAON HILLS

I would have written sooner. What to say?
I'm back? I'm home? The words, for me, are hard
to reconcile. I think about the way you move
from place to place, but Sargakhet is yours —
the woods where, each spring, rhododendron trees
bloom blood-red, drop their flowers on the road,
and, leaving them, require us to wonder
if paths are carpeted and soft, a gift,
or if we're trampling something we should cherish.

I love the red, the way the forests turn.
From far off, mixed with the oak, it isn't bright
as when, from underneath, it seems to glow.
Inside, the buds have iridescent streaks
like glitter left by elves — those forests could
be home to elves, wood nymphs, or goddesses
chasing each other, slipping away so fast
their sarees catch on branches, leaving tufts
of wedding color fixed to each hard snag.

To me, the paths all seemed to be the same,
each ridge, the stream we finally traveled to —
the one the next day might have been that stream —
but you could always walk us through and back
by stopping, glancing skyward, listening
to choiring pine or rustling hill bamboo,
a thousand years of voices in a temple,
a ceiling of silent bells, the sound of god —
I lose myself in all this, turn to wish —
the sound a wish makes — there, where you are home.

# THE LOST GIRLS
*Sargakhet*

*for my guide*

*You bring me to see the new land. I*
*will have to manage now myself. There's been*
*an accident, a sister, burned. You'll go*
*down to the plains to tend to her.*

Evening. The sun at angles on the paper-
white apple blossoms. The air taking the glow.
An old orchard, too-small trees, overgrown paths.
The pink-scrim twilight. What's behind it now?

Crows swarm, dive-bomb, then land down in the thatch
or perch. You say you haven't seen them flocked
like this for months. I want them gone, but you
wonder out loud why people don't like crows.

The sunset takes impossible dimensions
glowing white hot for too long on still clouds
until the silver linings etch on stone.
We leave before the day's clear light is gone —

down from the ridge, through nettle patches, brush
unclipped, then clipped, down past a cottage where
smoke curls gauzy threads — the evening meal.
A child escapes. A thin voice pulls her back.

—⚭—

*People see signs. Crows, ravens, dark clouds. I*
*misread the too-bright outlines — like eclipses'*
*coronas we know to avoid or blind*

*ourselves, like shattered glass, spilled mercury —*
*what seemed to be was not. I should have known.*
*I've seen the dead leave signposts on the sky —*
*wrong colors, shadows where the crows have flown.*

The woman on the path is angry
but I can't tell at whom, or why.
She speaks, and in your face, the change —
a page turned in the calendar.

—⁓—

                          Go back.
*Should I have seen a sign so many years*
*ago — when people told me stories? Then,*
*I wondered, but put the notes away, deleted*
*what I had written. It was fiction, and*
*I don't write fiction —*
                    *"In his house*
               *three sisters wait, invisible and silent —*
               *the oldest too … too everything: too tall,*
               *too beautiful, too smart, growing too old …"*

*or stories of story-ghosts. I should have asked —*
*"Your sisters?" — How to phrase it?*
                       *Would you have answered? —*
*"There's nothing to do about it. It just happened."*

—⁓—

None of it happened. Meeta was real. She married.

Here now —
        translating word to spoken word,
your English almost fails, then doesn't fail
at all — what other phrase? *She is no more.*

—⚊—

Her husband wants to keep some of the flowers.
He pleads for just a few to carry back,
something he can hold on to. He has lost
so much already in the accident —
a fire that never will seem just a fire —
that always will arouse some speculation.
But if they saw him here tonight, they'd know
there's nothing behind the story. Only this —

a young bride ripe with child, a small, bare kitchen,
a burner on the ground, the fumes, her clothes
draped as if waiting, ever, to ignite —
No intrigue. She lived long enough to tell.

Now, at the river, you must tell him *No* —
*for then she will be looking for her bones.*

—⚊—

You come back to the hills alone, your voice
like spider silk strung from the darkened branches:
*I thought I would be the one to bring her back.*

I want to say *There is still life here*, but
instead, I skirt around it, back away.

—∞—

*The baby was too beautiful. Eight months —*
*so perfect, even the doctor was unmoored.*

*The babies aren't cremated, only swaddled,*
*and taken to the river, to be left —*

The image only helps if, at the instant
she touches the surface, gods appear,
unwire our vision so that we can't see
her lifted to another river, somewhere —
where Meeta, now incarnate, waits for her.

—∞—

Why does your sister (I met her only once),
haunt me before and since? Was she too real —
your weeping mother too, two years hence, thin
as death itself (that's what you said) — her twin —
(another story) or your father?
                                        Still
at night, I see the baby girl alone
spun in the river's eddies —
                                        I can't tell
what branches hang above her —
                                        or if the crows

are flying towards her or retreating, or waiting —
or if she's safe, warm, dry —

                              even the moon
isn't a moon but months of pages turning
until the uncaught soul alights again.

# STILL LIFE

A handful of peaches on a burlap sack,
the sack itself, asafoetida salt,
a clean mud room, two more sacks for two beds,
garlic and onions strung like bride's bouquets,
a garland drying in the entryway
whose husks will fall, whose seeds will plant themselves —
the ceiling thatched, smoked black, and dry as bone
even in this monsoon. Outside, the stone
blue patio, the succulents arranged
in rusting cans with red geraniums,
the pathway lined with sunflowers, beckoning
towards clumps of dahlia so dark red they're black —
all this, and still the peaches on the ground
look most like love, and take me by surprise.

# HILL SOUNDS

As evening comes, cicadas start to tick
like footsteps — well, not footsteps. I'm projecting.
I want to hear you coming. I want to know
you noticed there was silence when I left.
The real sounds are: a family at day's end,
cicada's clicks, the barbet's bold, bright trills.

I've learned there are no secrets in the hills.
What's said down one slope's lifted and will wend
its way up to the next, with music's heft —
as clear as if, together, talking low,
we shared conspiracies. Now, I'm collecting
hill sounds to keep my growing fears in check.

But listening to the voices, I can't tell
if what's being said is kind or cruel. The tone
is different here. That's why I walked away
and let you be — the conversation pushed
to anger by inflections picked up wrong,
blown down the wrong steep slope by unseen wind.

It shouldn't be so hard for us to find
sounds that are true for both: the barbet's song
returned by his fair partner, in a hushed
repeat, not less, but called a different way,
so that they are distinct, but not alone;
or floodwaters after rain; or the temple bell.

# NIGHT SKY, WITH TELESCOPE
*Brooklyn*

September again. We've climbed up to the roof
to see the night's promised phenomena:
four moons of Jupiter, a quartered Venus,
but to the naked eye, they're only stars
slipped through the back-lit scrim of city haze.
Tonight, no constellations tell us stories
or draw a map to fix us to this place,
to home, the star that's always north, to truth
beyond the holy truths and holy laws.
Still, it's enough. Even from here, I see —
each heavenly body marks a switchback turn
or, like a tiny dot beside a number,
connects each house, each town, under one sky,
the villages we've lost to one another.

# ON THE NEW LAND, I WONDER

If earth's the only substance, molecules
of dust that hold a million other places,
composed of fragments without memory
themselves, but bound to everything that's been —

If land is patient, waiting like a mother
for her lost, angry child, her arms spread wide
only at that last moment, because she knew
before she saw you there that you would come—

If land turns into home when built upon.
If I will ever build here. If I do,
who else will build here, what will happen here —
so far from borders, once so far from time.

# NOTES

Cover: Like many of the "facts" in this book, the title itself is wrong. My father took this photograph in Srinagar in the early 1970s. He had it enlarged, and a huge print hung over the fireplace in our house in Pittsburgh, where I grew up. In 2007, I was told that the picture could not have been taken from Zero Bridge as I had always assumed, or imagined, or heard. In fact, there is no boat landing under Zero Bridge. The picture was probably taken from Amira Kadal.

"The Bandh" is the embankment that runs along the Jhelum River in Srinagar. *Bandh* in Hindi means *closed*, or *to close*.

"Eggs Burn Down House, Mother in Bar" is adapted from Catherine Bohne's prose. I am deeply grateful to her for letting me use her words, and for everything else she's given me.

The italicized "notes" in "The Story of the Palace" are taken from a number of web sites offering information about the architecture of Fatehpur Sikir, and from a guidebook I once used and have long since lost.

In "Brooklyn Botanic Gardens, 10/01," the italicized line is from Edgar Bowers' poem, "Ice Ages."

Phul Chunan is the name of the ceremony that takes place on the fourth morning after cremation, when the bones are picked from the cooled ashes of the funeral pyre. *Phul chunan* means *picking*, or *selecting the flowers*, in Punjabi.

The telescope man in "Neighboring Planet" is Joseph Delfausse.

# GLOSSARY

*chowkidar:* a night watchman

*kuddu:* a type of squash

*paise:* coins, like pennies

*panir piaz:* a dish of homemade cheese with onions

*rāg:* literally "color" or "mood," the series of musical notes on
 which the melody is founded in Indian classical music

*saag:* dark leafy greens, like spinach

*shikara:* a wooden boat

# ABOUT THE AUTHOR

Lynn Aarti Chandhok's poetry has appeared in *The New Republic*, *Tin House*, *The Antioch Review*, *The Hudson Review*, *The Missouri Review*, *Prairie Schooner*, and *Sewanee Theological Review*, on Poetry Daily, and in the anthology *Poetry Daily Essentials 2007*. In 2006, she received the Morton Marr Poetry Prize from the *Southwest Review*.

She was born and raised in Pittsburgh and spent childhood summers in Kashmir with her father's family. Educated at Swarthmore College and Tufts University, she has worked as a writer and as a middle and high school English teacher. She lives in Brooklyn, New York, with her husband, Robert Dieterich, and their daughters, Meena and Priya. She travels frequently to India.

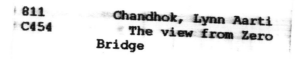